What Do You Think?

Has the Civil Rights Movement Been Successful?

John Meany

Heinemann Library
Chicago, Illinois

Editorial: Andrew Farrow and Rebecca Vickers
Design: Philippa Jenkins
Picture Research: Melissa Allison and Ruth Blair
Production: Alison Parsons

Originated by Heinemann Library
Printed and bound in China

13 12 11 10 09
10 9 8 7 6 5 4 3 2 1

Library of Congress Cataloging-in-Publication Data
Meany, John
  Has the civil rights movement been successful? / John Meany.
      p. cm. -- (What do you think?)
  Includes bibliographical references and index.
  ISBN 978-1-4329-1675-6 (hc)
  1. Civil rights movements--United States--History. 2. African Americans--Civil rights--History. 3.
United States--Race relations--History. 4. Racism--United States--History. I. Title.
  E185.61.M483 2008
  323.0973--dc22
                                        2008014756

Acknowledgments
The author and publishers are grateful to the following for permission to reproduce copyright
material: © Corbis pp. /Hulton-Deutsch Collection **28**, /Kamal Kishore/Reuters **42**, /Jason Reed/
Reuters **46**, /Reuters **38**, /Robert Sciarrino/Star Ledger **30**; © Getty Images pp. **44** /Paula Bronstein
18, /Charles Juba **11**, /Joe Raedle **23**, /Mark Wilson **6**, /Stone **20**, /Time & Life Pictures/Ellot Ellsofon
26, /Wireimage/Michael Caulfield **42**, /Wireimage/RJ Capak **36**; © Illustrated London News p. **4**;
© PA Photos pp. **8, 9, 10, 12, 24, 29, 31, 32, 37, 42, 44**, /AP Photo/Rich Pedroncelli **48**; © Kate
Shuster p. **14**.

Cover photograph of the leaders of the March on Washington, D.C. (August 28, 1963) reproduced
with permission of © Corbis/Bettman.

The publishers would like to thank Dr. Gwen Patton for her assistance in the preparation of this book.

Every effort has been made to contact copyright holders of any material reproduced in this book. Any
omissions will be rectified in subsequent printings if notice is given to the publisher.

Table Of Contents

Some words are printed in bold, **like this**. You can find out what they mean in the Glossary on pages 54–55.

> *Gandhi led the movement for independence in India*

Mohandas Gandhi lived during Britain's colonial control of India. He became a national leader, **protesting** against discriminatory British laws and for India's independence. His nonviolent struggle for India's freedom from the British Empire has been a model for civil rights organizations throughout the world. India earned independence in 1947.

The History Of The Civil Rights Movement

For thousands of years, individuals and societies have struggled for human freedom, equality, and justice. Governments and empires, great religions, and individual leaders called for human rights—the rights to life and property. Many societies in the past helped provide food, clothing, and shelter to the members of the common group. But few ancient or older communities had the kind of rights that people are concerned with today. There was little if any democracy. Many societies allowed citizens to keep slaves. Few had organized systems of justice or prohibitions against cruel and unusual punishment.

In England in 1215 the *Magna Carta*, which means "Great **Charter**," became the law. This series of charters, one of the most important legal documents in history, became the cornerstone of modern **civil rights**. The *Magna Carta* created a series of obligations or duties. It gave instructions to the leader of the country about how he could deal with the citizens. He was required to follow the law and to treat people fairly. The documents gave equal access to courts of law, stopped unlawful imprisonment, and required that individuals be tried by their **peers**. Since that time, the *Magna Carta* has influenced the development of laws and civil rights. Governments and citizens have added to these documents, creating modern civil rights.

> *Civil rights are based on the law*

Civil rights are the freedoms that an individual citizen or group has under the law. These rights vary from one country to another. These U.S. senators are considering proposals to limit the rights of prisoners held at Guantanamo Bay, Cuba, for reasons of national security.

The development of civil rights

During the past 200 years, there have been many instances of cruelty, discrimination, and violence directed at millions of people. To protect the victims of persecution and ill-treatment, many historical movements for social justice developed. These movements were well-organized groups with passionate leaders who argued for important economic, social, political, and legal reforms. Three major movements influenced the development of the modern **civil rights movement**. These were the movement to abolish slavery, the movement to organize support for women's suffrage (right to vote), and the movement to free countries from colonial rule.

Thomas Paine, the British-born **pamphleteer** of the American Revolution, published a pamphlet in 1775 entitled *African Slavery in America*. It called for the end of slavery:

> "As much in vain, perhaps, will they search ancient history for examples of the modern Slave-Trade. Too many nations enslaved the prisoners they took in war. But to go to nations with whom there is no war, who have no way provoked, without farther design of conquest, purely to catch inoffensive people, like wild beasts, for slaves, is an height of outrage against humanity and justice, that seems left by heathen nations to be practiced by pretended Christians. How shameful are all attempts to color and excuse it! As these people are not convicted of forfeiting freedom, they have still a natural, perfect right to it; and the governments whenever they come should, in justice set them free, and punish those who hold them in slavery."

The abolitionist movement

The organized slave trade had brought millions of Africans to the New World. A serious effort to end this cruel industry began in the late 18th century. Abolitionists formed antislavery groups, educated the public on the cruelty and dangers of slavery, and helped slaves escape to freedom. Although Britain outlawed the slave trade in 1807, the United States and other countries continued the practice.

The struggle over slavery was an important cause of the U.S. Civil War in the 1860s. During that war, President Abraham Lincoln issued the *Emancipation Proclamation*, freeing all slaves held in the rebelling states. This action was the beginning of the end for American slavery, but it did not guarantee equal treatment to freed slaves.

The suffrage movement

Democracy is a form of government with rules determined by the people of the country. Citizens are able to create and influence laws through free and fair elections. For many years prejudice against women denied them full participation in democracies by denying them the right to vote. The women's suffrage movement was an organized effort led by women to gain voting rights. Beginning in the mid-19th century in many countries, **suffragettes** protested in public and some were imprisoned. Eventually over time women have gained voting rights in most, but not all, countries.

The right to vote

In most countries women won full voting rights years after **universal suffrage** for men. The first country to grant full voting rights to women was New Zealand.

Country	Men vote	Women vote
New Zealand	1867	1893
United States	1870	1920
United Kingdom	1867	1928
France	1793	1944
Japan	1926	1946
Canada	1920	1960
Australia	1902	1962
Switzerland	1848	1971
Kuwait	1962	2005

World War II and the movement for civil rights

During World War II, more than 100 million people were involved in military operations throughout the world. With so many men involved in military combat and supply, new workers were needed for factories, farms, and businesses. The new workforce was made of people who had been left out of good jobs, mostly women and members of racial and ethnic minority groups. For these groups, new opportunities provided independence, self-respect, and higher wages. It also produced feelings of injustice and mistreatment. These groups began to realize that they should have always had the opportunities now open to them. In addition, members of minority groups joined the military. In the United States, more than one million Black soldiers from southern states participated. On returning home after being involved in the "global fight for freedom," they were still not allowed to vote. Excluded from society's economic, social, and political benefits, these groups began organizing to change society and the law. The civil rights movement's first goal was to eliminate legal **segregation**—the laws that prevented equal participation in society. Civil rights activists argued that these laws continued the immoral discrimination of slavery.

> **Nonviolent protest**

By refusing to follow a law that required Black citizens in Alabama to sit in the back of a city bus, Rosa Parks became a hero of the civil rights movement. Her arrest led to the Montgomery Bus Boycott, which encouraged people to rise up against laws that discriminated against African Americans.

> *Spiritual leadership in the civil rights movement*

The civil rights movement relied on the leadership of ministers from Black churches in the southern states. The Reverends Martin Luther King, Jr. and Ralph Abernathy helped form the Southern Christian Leadership Conference, a civil rights organization based on the religious principles of tolerance, respect, and the golden rule—treating others as you would like to be treated. This group became the core of civil rights protests and reforms.

Countries that had major roles in the war, for example, Britain and France, also had far-flung colonial empires. But these colonial powers had suffered enormous physical destruction and population losses leaving them economically and politically weakened. This gave opportunities for those living in the colonies to resist their foreign masters. Gandhi's nonviolent resistance to British rule in India was one example of this.

The stage is set for change

Social protestors, reformers, and politicians understood the successes and the limits of the history of civil rights up through World War II. The abolitionist, suffrage, and anti-colonial movements had generally been successful. Slavery was abolished. In most democracies women had the right to vote. Imperial rule was losing out and countries were returned to their own people for self-rule. At the same time, the discriminatory conditions for many people, especially for women and members of racial and ethnic minority groups, continued. For some it was difficult to get a quality education, good paying job, or decent place to live. Millions of citizens were discouraged or turned away when they tried to register to vote. More change was needed. The modern civil rights movement, which began in the United States during World War II, was an effort to reduce that discrimination. In addition to eliminating legal segregation, civil rights activists wanted respect and dignity. They wanted equal treatment.

Limited victories

The American civil rights movement of the 1940s–1970s was responsible for stopping legal discrimination. Court decisions ended the legal practice of segregation, or separation by race. New federal laws reduced job and housing discrimination. They also expanded the voting rights of African Americans and other groups. More government contracts were given to businesses that were owned and operated by minorities. The success of the civil rights movement encouraged international human and civil rights advances. Nearly 200 countries have signed the Universal Declaration of Human Rights, a UN-sponsored international agreement to protect the social and civil rights of people throughout the world. The issue for the 21st century is whether these new rules and laws will be enough to protect people against continued **stereotyping** and discrimination. This is still a troubling issue.

> *Civil rights for native peoples*

One growing area of the civil rights movement today involves attempts to protect indigenous peoples. These are the people that originally settled an area or have been living there for many generations. The Aboriginal peoples of Australia (as shown here), Native Americans in North America, and tribal groups in Africa and South America have found their lives and cultures threatened by environmental destruction and thoughtless economic development.

✔ Discrimination by opinions

Recent surveys by the National Opinion Research Center at the University of Chicago showed that more than 50% of the survey group of a cross-section of 1,200 Americans rated African Americans as less intelligent than Whites. More than 62% felt that they are lazier than their fellow White citizens, and 78% believed that African Americans preferred to live on welfare payments. This seems to show the continuing power of racial stereotypes.

Any group can claim civil rights

Any group can make the claim that it is victimized or subject to unequal treatment. The group can demand civil rights reform, so that its members are protected against social discrimination and hatred. There are new civil rights organizations for men and single people. Even 'outlaw' and hate groups, such as Nazi political organizations and White supremacists, argue that they do not get the respect and protection of the law that they are due.

Important events in the history of the civil rights movement

1863	**Emancipation Proclamation** *Order by President Abraham Lincoln during the Civil War frees all slaves in rebelling states.*
1948	**End of Segregation in U.S. Military** *Order by President Harry Truman integrates one of the country's largest organizations.*
1954	**Brown v. Board of Education of Topeka, Kansas** *Leading U.S. Supreme Court case, the decision of which rules that "separate educational facilities are ... unequal."*
1955	**Montgomery Bus Boycott** *Rosa Parks refuses to take a seat in the 'colored' section at the back of a bus. Her arrest for this action starts powerful civil rights protests against 'Jim Crow' laws.*
1963	**March on Washington, D.C.** *More than 200,000 people protest discrimination; Martin Luther King, Jr. delivers his "I Have a Dream" speech.*
1964	**Civil Rights Act** *New federal law ends discrimination based on race, national origin, religion, and color.*
1965	**Malcolm X assassinated**
1965	**Voting Rights Act** *Federal law encourages voter registration among minority groups.*
1968	**Martin Luther King, Jr. assassinated**
1992	**Race riots in Los Angeles** *This followed the acquittal of police officers accused of using excessive force when arresting African-American Rodney King for speeding.*

> *Civil rights leader used debating skills for his cause*

"Once my feet got wet, I was gone on debating. Whichever side of the selected subject was assigned to me, I'd track down and study everything I could find on it. I'd put myself in my opponents' place, and decide how I'd try to win if I had the other side; I'd figure a way to knock down all those points." Malcolm X, in *The Autobiography of Malcolm X* (1965)

Critical Thinking And Debating Skills

I ndividuals communicate to make sense of the world, share their ideas, and persuade people to support them. Using effective public speaking skills makes this work easier. Successful communicators make clear points, reduce misunderstandings, and influence others. How do they do it? They use verbal and nonverbal skills.

Verbal communication skills involve the effective use of one's voice. Is the speaker loud enough to be heard by the audience? Does the speaker change the pace of the speech, speeding up or slowing down to make it interesting for listeners? Does the speaker emphasize key words and phrases to remind the audience of important points, entertain them with humor, or carefully and effectively describe an idea? Does the speaker mumble or mispronounce words? The consistent use of the verbal skills of *volume*, *pace*, *emphasis*, and *clarity* help make for successful presentations.

Nonverbal skills, those that do not involve the voice, are also helpful. Good communicators make strong *eye contact* with an audience; they use head and hand *gestures* for emphasis. These skills are not difficult to understand, but they do require practice, particularly to use all of them throughout a presentation.

Argumentation

It is challenging to try to persuade others to consider a new idea. Why should they listen to a new one? To be persuasive, a person has to have a better idea. This encourages people to listen. They want the better idea—the one based on newer information, superior research and reasoning, and appeal to an audience. Better ideas can be expressed as **arguments**.

What is an argument? It is not just disagreement with another person. An argument is more than a simple opinion—it is the best possible expression of an opinion. It is both well reasoned and supported by evidence.

What are the parts of an argument?

An argument is an idea that includes an assertion, reasoning, and evidence. It is easy to identify an argument by the letters A-R-E, which represent its three parts, **a**ssertion, **r**easoning and **e**vidence. If it has A-R-E, it is an argument.

> *Public speaking*

Effective speakers learn to present information in clear, brief, entertaining, and persuasive ways. Public speaking is more than talking. A dynamic speaker must be knowledgeable and organized. Good public speakers have many common habits, but there is no "best" method for delivering an oral presentation. With training and practice, anyone can be an effective public speaker.

What is an assertion?

An assertion is the first part of an argument. It gives an opinion. It is a simple statement that a person will need to prove. Examples of assertions include:

- I am hungry.
- There should be universal voting rights.

What is reasoning?

The second part of an argument is reasoning. Reasoning is the analysis of an opinion. It is explanation of the assertion. It answers the question – WHY?

- WHY are you hungry?
- WHY should every adult have the right to vote?

What is evidence?

Evidence is the final part of an argument. It is the speaker's support for his or her reasoning. Evidence comes in many forms. It can be a historical or current example, a quotation from an expert, or statistics.

Sample arguments

Here are some examples of all of the parts of an argument: assertion, reasoning, and evidence (A–R–E).

I am hungry.
(Assertion) I am hungry. (Reasoning) I need to eat at scheduled meals to have energy throughout the day. (Evidence) But I had to miss lunch because I was busy finishing some homework.

There should be universal voting rights.
(Assertion) Every adult should have the right to vote. (Reasoning) Without the right to vote, a citizen does not have the ability to elect leaders or influence a government. If there is no voting, or if the right to vote is only held by a few people, then the general needs of the population will not be met.
(Evidence) Citizens want the right to vote. Those unable to vote argued for that right in suffrage movements that lasted decades. Once they got the vote, politicians had to take their views into account. Laws changed, making societies more equal. Universal voting has led in some places to universal education and fairer labor laws, as well as healthcare reforms and pension protection.

Argument conclusion

At the conclusion of an argument, an effective debater should be able to explain the reason that any single one of his or her arguments is more important than the combined total of all the opposing arguments. So, any one argument for one side should be able to stand up against all the arguments for the other side.

> *Voting rights*

Democratic government is based on voting—the right of the people to be involved in the affairs of government through elections. Voting is necessary to influence political leaders. It also protects other rights of citizenship—the rights to free speech and press, equality, and religion. Voting rights are the foundation of civil rights.

The Civil Rights Movement And Legal Reform

Racial segregation in the United States involved the physical separation of the races. Racial separation in some localities was approved and enforced by the rule of law. This form of discrimination is known as "***de jure***" segregation. Laws made it difficult for anyone other than White males to vote, attend school, or find jobs. Laws segregated neighborhoods, hospitals, hotels, restaurants, movie theaters, public transportation, public restrooms, and even water fountains. Arizona and Wyoming prohibited interracial marriage. The Wyoming law read: "All marriages of White persons with Negroes, Mulattos, Mongolians, or Malays hereafter contracted in the State of Wyoming are and shall be illegal and void." Georgia had separate mental health facilities. Florida had separate schools. Some states, such as Louisiana, required that circuses and theaters have separate entrances and seating. Oklahoma did not permit integrated swimming. North Carolina segregated its public libraries. Mississippi made it a crime to speak out in favor of equality.

The immediate goal of the civil rights movement was to overturn these laws and end racial segregation. But there was an additional goal of the movement. The civil rights movement was also dedicated to fair treatment—its leaders did not just expect equal opportunity, but wanted to achieve equal results.

✔ What are *de jure* and *de facto* discrimination?

It is possible for some discrimination to occur under the law. This is also known as *de jure* discrimination. *De jure* is a Latin phrase that means "by law." When slavery was legal, it was *de jure* discrimination. The denial of voting rights, the **Black Codes**, and **Jim Crow laws** on segregation were other examples of *de jure* discrimination. An equally powerful form of unequal treatment is *de facto* discrimination. *De facto* is a Latin phrase that means, "by fact," rather than by law. *De facto* discrimination describes what really is happening to people, regardless of what the law says. It explores the facts. If discrimination is outlawed, but it still occurs, it is *de facto* discrimination.

Using the law

The law has often been an important tool for social reform. The U.S. Constitution was repeatedly amended to promote civil rights. The Thirteenth Amendment abolished slavery. The Fourteenth Amendment granted citizenship to any person born within the United States. In addition, this amendment protected the rights of individuals against the discriminatory decisions of individual states. The Fifteenth Amendment guaranteed the right to vote, regardless of race or color. There were additional laws that added to civil rights, including the Voting Rights Act of 1965. With more access to the political process, the number of African Americans in political leadership positions dramatically increased. The Joint Center for Political and Economic Studies noted in its 2003 report, *Black Elected Officials: A Statistical Summary*, that in 1970, there were only 1,469 Black Americans serving as elected officials. Thirty years later, there were more than 9,000.

Is it enough to eliminate segregationist laws?

In describing the National Association for the Advancement of Colored People (NAACP), the nation's leading civil rights organization, Carole Cannon, a reporter in Akron, Ohio wrote: "Critics say the organization is a dinosaur whose national leadership is still living in the glory days of the civil rights movement." Cannon went on to quote Dr. Frederick Zak, a young local NAACP president, who said: "There is a tendency by some of the older people to romanticize the struggle— especially the marching and the picketing and the boycotting and the going to jail." Former NAACP President Dr. Benjamin Hooks believes that the perilous times of the civil rights movement should never be taken for granted, especially by those who were born in the aftermath of the movement's gains. "A young Black man can't understand what it means to have something he's never been denied", Hooks told *U.S. News and World Report*. Whose opinion seems right?

Can diversity cause policy changes?

If more members of minority ethnic groups are elected to public office, do you think it will produce change? Can you support your opinion using A-R-E? Check out these opinions:

✔ **For**—*More diversity among officials will produce more diverse laws*
"... African Americans and women serving in state legislatures are significantly more likely to introduce "Black interest" and "women interest" legislation. This provides strong empirical support for the notion that...representation, or the legislative composition in government, directly impacts...the policy interests of the electorate."

D'Andra Orey and Christopher Larimer, professors of political science, University of Nebraska–Lincoln

✔ **Against**—*Government does not change simply because of diversity*
"Historically entrenched racial, ethnic, and gender discrimination has been challenged and the presence of previously underrepresented groups in the policy-making process has modestly expanded as a result. The broader claims for establishing universal social rights and delivering substantive political and economic equality to all citizens lacked the intense support of powerful groups... The consequence is that rising economic inequality has neither expanded nor reduced political inequality nor even produced a dramatic redirection of overall government policy in the egalitarian or anti-egalitarian direction."

Task Force on Inequality and American Governance, American Political Science Association

Do affirmative action policies help or hurt civil rights?

Affirmative action programs are steps to correct past discrimination by encouraging equal opportunity. Civil rights groups generally support them, but they are controversial. Do you think affirmative action is fair? Does it promote civil rights?

Opinions for affirmative action	Opinions against affirmative action
Encourages diversity in schools and the workplace	Discriminates against qualified individuals
Corrects past and present discrimination	Hurts minorities by labeling them as "affirmative action" students or employees
Has a history of success in including women and people of color, helping civil rights	Hurts civil rights by looking at race and gender, rather than merit

> *Internment in the United States during World War II*

After Japan's surprise attack on the U.S. fleet at the Pearl Harbor naval base in 1941, and the declaration of war with Japan, national security concerns led to the imprisonment of more than 100,000 people of Japanese heritage living in the western United States. Citizens and recent immigrants lost homes, businesses, and jobs.

✔ Using the law to limit civil rights

Throughout history, the law has been used to protect one group by denying rights to another. Each wave of immigration to the United States seems to have led to anti-immigration laws and policies, including the Chinese Exclusion Act (1882), Executive Order 9066 (1942) for **Japanese internment**, and Operation Wetback (1954) for the forced removal of a million illegal Mexican immigrants. More recently, new local laws have been directed against immigrants, including ones that make English the official language, ban foreign flags, and attempt to limit housing and employment for undocumented immigrants. Some states, such as Michigan and California, have banned affirmative action in public education and employment.

Can you think of laws that restrict the freedom and rights of a particular group? Do you think these are fair?

African-American leaders debate affirmative action

"There's nothing wrong in concept with affirmative action as the idea that you make up for discrimination that has taken place by reaching out to people. And in some cases where you have equal qualified people taking the people with less."

Mary Frances Berry, former chair of the U.S. Commission on Civil Rights

"Government-sanctioned discrimination to engineer racial and gender 'representation' in various fields is not a good policy for America."

Ward Connerly, former member of the University of California Board of Regents

New laws can improve the lives of people; they can also reduce opportunities for social equality. Examine the following legal reforms and consider whether they improve public policy or might be an example of *de jure* discrimination.

Bilingual education

Three states—California, Massachusetts, and Arizona—have banned bilingual education. These states have more than half of the U.S. population of students who speak a language other than English in the home. Supporters of the bilingual ban claim that it is not discriminatory, saying that English-only language instruction is a valid and helpful educational policy. Opponents argue that the ban unfairly targets minority students and hurts their educational and employment opportunities. Is the law fair? What do you think?

Redistricting

A district is a geographic area in which a person can legally vote. In most states, districts are set by state legislatures. In the United States, the law requires that each political district should have approximately the same population size as other districts. Politicians have changed these political boundaries through a practice called redistricting. In some cases, redistricting has reduced the political influence and voting power of ethnic minority groups. For example, if a region had a Black majority, it could be divided up into other districts with high White populations. Supporters of redistricting claim that each vote is equally important. Opponents have argued that race should be considered when drawing district borders to guarantee that there is ethnic minority representation in government. Is race-based redistricting fair? What do you think?

Public education—a civil right

For many decades, African Americans and other minority groups were denied the right to a quality education in American public schools. They were denied the chance to learn to read, write, and become productive citizens. School segregation made adult discrimination more possible. If African Americans were uneducated, they could not qualify for good paying jobs. If they could not read, they could not complete the paperwork to buy houses or start businesses.

Court decisions in the 1950s and 1960s ended legal school segregation. But many Whites chose to move their homes to racially segregated neighborhoods. According to the 2005 report of the Children's Defense Fund, *The State of America's Children*, 71 percent of Black students attend low performing schools where the majority of students are members of ethnic minorities. The U.S. Department of Education's 2006 education statistics noted that only 25 percent of students from ethnic minorities had the reading and math skills of White students. Has another form of bias replaced *de jure* segregation?

Landmark Supreme Court decisions on equal education

Plessy v. Ferguson, 1896
Homer Plessy was arrested and convicted for refusing to move from a railway car that was "for whites only." He appealed his conviction to the Supreme Court. The court decided against him, ruling that racial segregation in "separate but equal" conditions was permitted. This decision made segregation legal under the U.S. Constitution.

Brown v. Board of Education of Topeka, Kansas, 1954
African-American parents were denied the right to educate their children in neighborhood schools in Topeka, Kansas. The children could only attend one of the four schools for African Americans in the city. The parents sued to open public education to all students. In 1954, this Supreme Court decision supported them. The decision overturned the *Plessy* case—the Supreme Court ruled that separate facilities were never equal, that "separate is inherently… unequal."

Meredith v. Jefferson County Board of Education, 2007
In 2007, in a 5-4 decision, the Supreme Court reduced the power of the *Brown* decision. It ruled that race could not be used by school districts in student assignment, even to promote diversity. Although this does not approve segregated schools, the decision may prevent school leaders from moves to integrate segregated schools.

Educational opportunity—the right of all children

"Today, education is perhaps the most important function of state and local governments. Compulsory school attendance laws and the great expenditures for education both demonstrate our recognition of the importance of education to our democratic society. It is required in the performance of our most basic public responsibilities, even service in the armed forces. It is the very foundation of good citizenship. Today it is a principal instrument in awakening the child to cultural values, in preparing him for later professional training, and in helping him to adjust normally to his environment. In these days, it is doubtful that any child may reasonably be expected to succeed in life if he is denied the opportunity of an education. Such an opportunity, where the state has undertaken to provide it, is a right which must be made available to all on equal terms."

Chief Justice Earl Warren, Brown v. Board of Education, 1954

> *Schools can help race relations*

Can schools help to foster positive attitudes about race? Researchers at the University of Texas found that education about historical discrimination and struggles with racism significantly improved White children's positive attitudes towards all African Americans. But attending an integrated school does not improve acceptance of African American and other minority children if within the school classes remain segregated.

Voting rights—the foundation of democracy

The first American voting rights were based on property ownership. If an individual had property, that person also had the right to vote. Because few minorities or women were permitted to own property, few had the ability to vote. The 14th and 15th Amendments to the U.S. Constitution permitted more people to vote, but state governments, particularly in the southern states, often added barriers to voting. These included the poll tax, "grandfather" laws, and literacy tests. The poll tax was a tax on each person who had the right to vote. Because segregation prevented African Americans from getting good paying jobs or starting businesses, many were unable to pay the tax. Grandfather laws or clauses required that the applicant, in order to register to vote, needed to prove that his or her grandfather had been a registered voter. For most African Americans in the South, this was not the case. Literacy tests tried to make sure that each voter could read and write. This may seem fair. No country wants ignorant voters. But African Americans and other groups were denied the right to education. It was not fair to both deny people the opportunity to get an education and then use their failure to get an education to prevent them from voting. Even when an applicant passed all the literacy requirements they could be asked impossible questions, such as "How many seeds are in a watermelon?" or "How many bubbles are in a bar of soap?" In the 19th century, freed Blacks used their new voting rights. Because of literacy tests and poll taxes, by 1900 virtually no African Americans in the South were able to vote.

> *Choosing nonviolence or armed resistance to discrimination*

Many leading civil rights organizations used the methods of nonviolent resistance and **civil disobedience**. Other organizations, such as the **Black Panther Party**, argued that armed defense might be necessary in the struggle to achieve equality.

In 1965, more than a century after the Emancipation Proclamation, the U.S. Congress passed the Voting Rights Act, permitting all citizens to register and vote. Without the right to vote, the people have no say about any other right or opportunity.

Voting differences based on race

The U.S. Census Bureau reported in 2004 that 69% of eligible Black voters were registered to vote. This compares with 74% of White voters. In the 2004 elections, 60% of registered Black voters actually voted, compared to 65% of White voters. Has the civil rights movement succeeded in ensuring an equal right and ability to vote?

Nonviolent protest and armed resistance

The majority of civil rights organizations used nonviolence to achieve their goals. They were led by the instruction and example of the Reverend Dr. Martin Luther King, Jr. Dr. King was a minister who preached the value of peaceful, but determined, action. He not only opposed the use of violence, but also knew that his movement would not get sympathy if it used violence against government leaders, the police, and business owners. The main tactic was civil disobedience. Civil disobedience has three requirements:

- It is an illegal act.
- It has a political message.
- It is nonviolent.

King and other civil rights leaders organized protest marches, sit-ins at restaurants that denied service to Blacks, and bus boycotts (refusal to ride on segregated buses or ones that forced Blacks to sit in the back).

Nonviolent protests were supported, in part, by threats of violence. These did not come from the major nonviolent civil rights organizations, but from groups supporting armed resistance and self-defense to counter White violence. One of the main leaders of these groups was Malcolm X, founder of the Black Muslim group, the Nation of Islam, who declared that African Americans should get pride, self-respect, and equal treatment "by any means necessary." Other organizations, such as Louisiana's "Deacons of Defense and Justice," a military style self-defense organization, provided armed security for nonviolent civil rights protestors. The majority of Americans feared the threat of violence and rioting. The nonviolence movement gave interested and committed members of the public a safe and legal way to participate in events that aimed to change laws and increase civil rights. Is nonviolence always best? Can violence be justified to promote equality? What do you think?

> *Bob Marley*

Born into the poverty and slums of Kingston, Jamaica, Bob Marley became a global leader in the struggle for civil rights and social equality. One of the most popular musical performers of all time, he inspired millions with songs that encouraged people to stand up for their rights, resist discrimination, and work to end segregation.

The Civil Rights Movement And Popular Culture

Artists are often the people in a community who push the boundaries of creativity and change. Sometimes their new ideas involve them in political and social controversies serious enough to lead to discrimination and even imprisonment. The period of the development of the civil rights movement from the 1940s to the 1970s was a time of enormous growth in media and mass popular culture. At the end of the 1940s, few people owned a television. Only a few dozen cities offered any television programming. By the end of the 1950s, however, almost every American watched television. News and entertainment broadcasts brought the world into people's homes. In news stories, television showed the injustice and indignity of segregation to a larger audience, while its entertainment programs featured Black entertainers and sports stars. These stars often developed popular followings among White fans. When these entertainers and sports stars supported the cause of civil rights reform, they gained the support of many of their fans for the cause.

Musicians, writers, artists, filmmakers, athletes, and actors, Black and White, participated in the civil rights movement. They marched with Martin Luther King, Jr., delivered speeches for social justice, raised money for civil rights organizations, and used civil rights themes and stories in their works.

Music—Jim Crow to gospel choirs

During the 19th century, aspects of popular entertainment helped contribute to negative images of slaves, and, later, of free Blacks. White performers wearing make-up to give them black faces were a popular form of entertainment. They performed on riverboats and in minstrel shows, which included singing, dancing, and comedy. Shows like these produced a negative and ignorant view of Black people. Among the popular entertainers in the 1830s was White performer T. D. Rice, who sang the comical song, "Jumpin' Jim Crow" wearing blackface make-up. This song, with its negative depiction of an inferior and unintelligent Black man, later gave its name to the deep-South laws that supported racial segregation, the so-called Jim Crow laws.

In the years following World War II, a connection developed between the civil rights movement and entertainment, originating in the movement's religious leadership in the southern states. Many African American civil rights activists were preachers, and a popular form of music in the Black churches of the South was gospel music, which was used during the religious services. Gospel singers, groups, and choirs began to write and perform songs with civil rights themes. The music was also used to entertain audiences that gathered for protest marches. Additionally, protestors often sang while marching—their voices gave them courage and a feeling that they had a shared mission. In the North, mainly White supporters of the civil rights movement also wrote and performed civil rights songs in folk clubs and on college campuses.

> The integration of sports

The U.S. civil rights movement opened opportunities for members of ethnic minority groups and women to participate in the careers, live in neighborhoods, and attend educational establishments that had excluded them in the past. Many organized sports had, by rule or custom, prohibited integrated participation by Black athletes. It was not until 1950 that Althea Gibson broke the "color line" in tennis. She was the first Black winner of Wimbledon (1957) and the U.S. Nationals (1957), and, after 11 Grand Slam title wins, was the first Black person inducted into the International Tennis Hall of Fame.

Songs of Freedom

Throughout history, music has been used to gather, organize, and inspire people. This was also true of the songs in the civil rights movement. Some lyrics describe injustices, others tell the stories of civil rights struggles, like The Staples Singers' tale of the protest march from Selma to Montgomery, Alabama, "March Up Freedom's Highway." Here is another example:

```
"I go to the movie and I go downtown
Somebody keeps telling me don't hang around
It's been a long, a long time coming
But I know, a change is gonna come."

[Sam Cooke, "A Change is Gonna Come"]
```

The benefits and costs of gansta rap

In the past decade, some have argued that Black images in music and film have gone too far. They have argued that the appearance of Black men as gangsters undermines the achievements of civil rights. What do you think? Has gangsta rap, for example, done more harm than good? Do the lyrics of gangsta rap point up the successes or failures of the civil rights movement?

Is gangsta rap a positive expression of civil rights?

"Through radio air play, these young men attained visibility from an otherwise marginalized existence in America. In fact, Rap would be proclaimed as the Black CNN. Many rappers gave voice to what would have otherwise remained unseen by the larger dominant American public: police brutality, poverty, and urban deterioration. With its confrontational style, Rap defied both Black and White middle class norms. Rappers spoke in their own voice and on their own terms, as members of a historically marginalized segment of America's population living in America's blighted urban areas."

Akilah Folami, law professor

"We have got to get out of this gangster mentality, acting as if gangsterism and blackness are synonymous. I think we have allowed a whole generation of young people to feel that if they're focused, they're not Black enough. If they speak well and act well, they're acting White, and there's nothing more racist than that."

Rev. Al Sharpton, minister and civil rights activist

The entertainment industry and civil rights

Support for civil rights came from every part of the entertainment industry. Actors and writers traveled to the South during the **Mississippi Freedom Summer Project** to bring cultural activities and other education opportunities. Actress Ruby Dee established a group, Artists and Writers for Justice, which began a **boycott** of businesses in Birmingham, Alabama after four African American girls were killed in a bombing there. Several civil rights organizations were able to hire full time staff due to the fundraising of successful celebrities. But some entertainers were stopped from giving whole-hearted, personal support. Owners of music and film companies did not want controversy or political identification to hurt their businesses. Some were worried about upsetting White consumers, particularly in southern states. Performers, Black and White, could not be too outspoken and continue successful careers. Also, civil rights leaders did not want their movement dominated by celebrities. They understood that artists, comedians, actors, musicians, and writers had media connections that could increase publicity for their cause. But they were also concerned that it might be the wrong kind of publicity and that it could make the issues look less serious. As a result, many entertainers worked in the background of the civil rights movement.

Girl power?

Many in the entertainment industry, including writers, actors, and musicians, were actively involved in the civil rights movement. Plays, television programs, films, and songs described the fight for social justice, freedom, and civil rights. Some goals of the civil rights movement were later used as much for advertising as for the universal struggle for human dignity and rights. For example, do you think that the Spice Girls "Girl Power" slogan helped empower girls and young women in the late 1990s in a good way or was it simply organized by producers as a clever way to market the group to audiences? Can this kind of use demean and trivialize the serious point of the slogan? Do you think it is a little of both, a gimmick that also encouraged gender equality and independence?

Has the civil rights movement had an impact on popular culture?

From the time of the minstrel shows, there is no question that there has been a dramatic change in popular entertainment. Many people from groups that faced discrimination and segregation in the past have become famous, wealthy, and admired from their participation in entertainment and sports. But the success is mixed. Even today, in the United States few African Americans

> *Protest at the Olympics*

The politics of civil rights gained an audience throughout the world during the 1968 Summer Olympic Games in Mexico City. American track stars Tommie Smith and John Carlos raised their fists in a salute to "Black Power" and an end to discrimination just before receiving their gold and bronze medals.

appear on television as professionals—as newsmakers, experts, or journalists. Blacks are generally excluded from popular television and film programming. The National Association of Black Journalists reported that of those making policy decisions, 93 percent of television general managers are White and 80 percent are male. They noted that only 22 percent of television's journalists are from ethnic minorities, significantly lower than the percentage of the ethnic minority population (33 percent). In sports the Wolfers-Price study of May 2007 showed that basketball referees called more fouls on Black players than White players. The rules may seem fair, but does hidden discrimination still interfere with real equality?

 ## The end of the color barrier in professional baseball

Baseball is one of the most popular sports in the United States. Originally, in the 19th century, mixed Black and White teams played. Later Black athletes were banned from integrated teams. They played in the separate Negro League. In 1947, the color barrier was broken when Jackie Robinson joined the Brooklyn Dodgers. Robinson was not only a talented baseball player, but was also a fierce competitor. Named to the Baseball Hall of Fame, he became a model for the integration of sports in the United States and throughout the world. In his later years, Robinson worked on civil rights reforms and wrote letters of support for Martin Luther King, Jr. and Malcolm X.

> *Stereotyping and hidden prejudice*

What is your general impression of a "terrorist?" Public polls show that many people associate terrorists with those who are Middle Eastern, male, and young. This is a **stereotype**—a general impression of the qualities of an individual or group. Does your mental image of what a terrorist looks like match these members of Aum Shinrikyo, a Japanese religious cult responsible for a subway nerve gas attack in Tokyo that killed 12 people and injured thousands? Does it match the Midwestern White men, veterans of the U.S. Army, convicted for the murder of 168 people in the 1995 bombing of Oklahoma City's Murrah Building?

Stereotyping And Private Discrimination

Stereotyping is a way of labeling or describing an individual or group. In stereotyping, the focus is in thinking about general categories, rather than about the very specific details of each person. This makes the world simpler and easier to understand and explain, but it is also less accurate. Stereotypes often miss the unique, special, and individual characteristics of a person or group. General impressions based on a person's race, ethnicity, gender, nationality, religion, or age are likely to be wrong when applied to an individual.

Stereotypes of groups are difficult to eliminate from people's thinking. They are created and reinforced by messages that are received every day from governments, businesses, mass media, and friends. Some stereotypes are favorable. Groups can be described as "hard-working," "honest," and "friendly." But more importantly, the impressions that are created and shared through stereotypes are often negative. The struggle against negative stereotyping has been part of the movement for civil rights and equal treatment. It was negative stereotyping of Black people that contributed to slavery, segregation, and discrimination. Although there has been a significant amount of legal civil rights reform, negative stereotyping continues to this day. It can interfere with equal and fair treatment for all.

Personal prejudices

The overwhelming majority of people like to believe, in general, that they are honest, fair, and good. Few people would describe themselves as "racist," "sexist," or "anti-immigrant." It is the case, however, that the majority of the public believe in and use negative stereotypes. The opinions of trusted friends and family, as well as the news and information from the mass media and national political and business leaders, shape these attitudes and opinions.

Legal discrimination has been outlawed in many democratic societies. It is not legal to own or trade slaves. There is a nearly universal right of adult citizens to vote. Individuals charged with a crime generally have the protection of due process, a right to be treated fairly. Many countries have legal protection to guarantee equal opportunity for an education, health care, housing, and employment. But private discrimination and personal prejudices may have also increased. Prejudice, for example, was behind the historical decision in some places to have separate school systems for Black and White children. The Supreme Court decision in *Brown v. Board of Education* eliminated legal segregation but it could not change people's attitudes. Brown forced schools to open their doors to Black children, but it could not force White students to stay in the same schools. More than fifty years after the Brown decision, White students in some areas have left public education and attend private schools. Although public education is open to all, many public schools are now as segregated as they were in the days before the *Brown* decision.

Does segregation continue?

Gary Orfield, the Co-Director of Harvard University's Civil Rights Project, reported that 71 percent of African Americans attend a school that is predominantly nonwhite while only 11 percent of White students do so. Has education really been made open and accessible? Is it still "separate but equal" or is it just "separate"?

"There is nothing magic about sitting next to a child of another race. But if we ask 'Is there a difference between being in an impoverished school or a middle-class school?', there's a huge difference."

Gary Orfield, Professor of Education Co-Director Harvard University Civil Rights Project.

Do you think there is anything wrong with segregated education? Are there any arguments to be made in favor of segregation? What about same-sex classes or schools? Are they justified? Is it acceptable to segregate students based on test scores or language abilities, even if this might increase racial and ethnic segregation? What about religious schools? Should they be integrated with members of other religions or atheists?"

✔ Do you stereotype?

> "All stereotypes turn out to be true. This is a horrifying thing about life. All those things you fought against as a youth: you begin to realize they're stereotypes because they're true."
> *David Cronenberg (1943–), film director*

> "Instead of being presented with stereotypes by age, sex, color, class, or religion, children must have the opportunity to learn that within each range, some people are loathsome and some are delightful."
> *Margaret Mead (1901–1978), anthropologist*

Personal civil rights reform

What image comes to mind when you think of a "business leader," a "professional athlete," or a "criminal?" For a business leader do you think of Mark Zuckerberg, the college-age billionaire owner of Facebook? Is the professional athlete you think of young Asian-American Michelle Wie, the world's highest paid female golfer? Is your image of a criminal 64-year-old Conrad Black, the wealthy Canadian media executive convicted of criminal fraud? The first step in personal civil rights reform is to identify your own **biases** and stereotypes. Once they are identified, it is then possible to examine them, learn from them, and change them.

Profile 1
- From a poor, urban environment
- History of drug and alcohol use
- Criminal convictions
- Single parent home
- Criticized for lyrics that promote violence
- Hip hop performer

Profile 2
- Trained as a figure skater
- Studied to be a concert pianist
- Gained a PhD at the age of 26 with a dissertation on military policy and politics in Czechoslovakia
- Professor at Stanford University
- Converses in Russian, German, French, and Spanish

Think about the stereotype that you have for the people profiled above. Make a mental image of each person. Then turn the page. Did you guess correctly?

> **Profile 1: Eminem**

Eminem (Marshall Mathers), one of the world's leading hip hop artists and music producers, has sold more than 70 million records. He starred in *8 Mile*, a movie loosely based on the story of his life. Eminem has won nine Grammy Awards, one Academy Award, and more than 25 other major awards for his music.

> **Profile 2: Condoleezza Rice**

In 2005, Dr. Condoleezza Rice became the first African-American woman appointed to be the U.S. Secretary of State. Prior to this appointment, Dr. Rice had served for five years as Presidential National Security Advisor. During her time at Stanford University, she served as Provost (head academic administrator) from 1993 to 1999. Dr. Rice was the first woman, and first member of a minority ethnic group, to hold this post.

Measuring success

Personal prejudices and stereotypes may be hard to change. But how far have things come for African Americans in those areas that can be more easily measured? How far is there still to go? Many statistics seem to show that little has changed in the past several decades.

The 2007 *National Urban League Equality Index* compares lifestyles and living conditions for Black and White Americans. It concluded that African Americans are paid less for the same work, have double the rate of unemployment, and are three times as likely to live in poverty. The average lifespan of a Black person is five years less than for a White person and, in general, the Black person is more likely to be unhealthy during his or her life. Black men are six times more likely than White men to be imprisoned. They are less likely to receive a quality education or to have similar educational achievement. In only one category were African Americans better off—they were more likely to be active members of their communities, as measured by voting, union activity, and volunteerism.

Which type of discrimination is most challenging to solve?

Examine this list and identify which are examples of *de jure* discrimination and which are *de facto* discrimination (see box on page 18).

✔ A state requires a tax to register to vote
✔ Black workers are paid less than White workers
✔ "Whites only" water fountains
✔ Neighbors oppose interracial dating
✔ The FBI targets Middle Eastern men for racial profiling
✔ Hotel will not rent rooms to Black guests
✔ Students attend a school with an overwhelmingly majority Black population
✔ Slow service for Black customers in a restaurant

Which discriminatory practices would be the hardest to change? Why?

"The problem with *de facto* segregation is that it allows for discrimination to occur much easier. All black neighborhoods and all black schools are targets for neglect of services and unequal funding. Our challenge is to devise strategies that will make real the dreams and the struggles of those courageous pioneers, white and black, who fought for a one America; those who struggled to remove the veil of Jim Crow; those who fought to end segregated housing patterns that would go a long way to end *de facto* segregation."

Freddie Parker, Professor of African-American History, North Carolina Central University
[http://72.14.253.104/search?q=cache:AwF_8jfrh5IJ:www.dlt.ncssm.edu/lmtm/docs/de_segregation/script.doc+examples+of+de+facto+discrimination&hl=en&ct=clnk&cd=57&gl=us]

> Race and the Katrina disaster

In 2005, Hurricane Katrina swept in from the Gulf of Mexico, devastating the city of New Orleans and much of the coastline. Days after the disaster, the federal government still had not helped solve the humanitarian crisis. Did the fact that the hundreds of thousands of victims were mostly African American affect the government's response? Is it an example of the failure of the civil rights movement that the poor and Black communities in New Orleans seemed abandoned and unprotected in the aftermath of the storm?

Case Study: Hurricane Katrina

An examination of the circumstances in New Orleans after Hurricane Katrina may provide a way to investigate the nature of race relations, equal rights under the law, and private discrimination. The effects of the civil rights movement improved the living and working conditions for people in the Gulf region. The African-American mayor of New Orleans was also able to speak out and help the city's Black community. His election, which put him in a position to give political and economic support to poor, Black residents who were victims of the storm, would have been unlikely without voting rights reform. So the elimination of *de jure* discrimination helped the victims of Katrina. At the same time, there may have been significant *de facto* discrimination. For financial reasons, much of New Orleans' Black community was unable to flee the storm. Since the clean up started, little government support to rebuild Black areas of the city materialized. However, tens of thousands of evacuated African Americans were welcomed into White homes throughout the country, and hundreds of millions of dollars in private, charitable aid was donated to the Black community. Has the civil rights movement succeeded here, based on its original goals of ending legal segregation and producing equal treatment? Has *de facto* discrimination become more important than *de jure* segregation?

In the aftermath

Hurricane Katrina destroyed homes and businesses, flooded city streets, killed many hundreds of people, and led to the evacuation of hundreds of thousands more. But many residents of the region thought that race played a role in the way the disaster was handled. Many Black residents were unable to flee the storm. Civil rights activist Professor Michael Eric Dyson commented:

> "Even among the oppressed, however, there are stark differences. Concentrated poverty doesn't victimize poor whites in the same way that it does poor blacks. For instance, the racial divide in car ownership discussed earlier partially reflects income difference between the races.
>
> "However, as if to prove that not all inequalities are equal, even poor whites are far more likely to have access to cars than poor blacks. In New Orleans, 53% of poor blacks were without cars while just 17% of poor whites lacked access to cars... It is bad enough to be white and poor; it is worse still to be black, or brown, or female, and young, and poor. Simply said, race makes class hurt more."

In a *Washington Post*/ABC News poll, about 60 percent of African Americans thought that race was a factor in the government's delayed emergency response. The predominantly White Mississippi residents, who were affected by Katrina, received more government and private recovery aid than did the Black residents of New Orleans.

Problems fighting de facto segregation

De facto discrimination appears to be a continuing problem. John Logan, a sociologist at Brown University, estimated in 2006 that 20 percent of New Orleans' residents, hundreds of thousands of people, the majority of whom are Black, will not return to their home or city.

The Southern Poverty Law Center's *Tolerance.org* website tracked a number of false stories during the hurricane emergency, including several that stereotyped Black residents as looters and criminals. Alphonso Jackson, U.S. Secretary of Housing and Urban Development, admitted that the New Orleans' White residential neighborhoods and business areas were being rebuilt, but that was not the case for many Black-majority neighborhoods. But the city's leader was African American.

The majority of the affected residents were also poor. What do you think? Were the problems of Hurricane Katrina about poverty or did race matter? Has civil rights reform in the region generally succeeded or has it failed to meet its most important goal of equality?

> *Isolated Black prisoners the last taken to safety*

Human Rights Watch charged that prisoners in the New Orleans county jail, the majority of whom were black, were abandoned during the Hurricane Katrina flooding. The prisoners were left without food, water, or electricity; some were still locked in their cells. Inmates were eventually taken to safety, some after the floodwaters had reached neck-high.

> *National security protection of civil rights*

National security does not always threaten civil rights. It is often in the interest of a government to protect citizens' rights, such as the right to vote. In some countries and at particular times in history, it has been necessary to have military and police forces guard polling places and voting booths to guarantee that all registered voters who wanted to could do so. It also prevents illegal actions, such as people trying to vote more than once or intimidating others to vote in a certain way. These people are being searched as they wait to vote in the first multiparty elections in over 40 years in the Democratic Republic of the Congo.

Will National Security Needs Slow Civil Rights Reforms?

C ivil rights are the freedoms, protections, and opportunities that citizens have according to the law. During national emergencies or war, however, the law and civil rights can change. During a national crisis, the general public is more concerned with safety than with freedom or equality. They are more concerned with the protection of the larger group, not the need to give rights to a minority of the population. In the interest of national security, a country might limit immigration or restrict the movement of people within its border. The government may increase its power to investigate citizens, particularly the ones who disagree with government policy. Political parties and organizations may be outlawed and the members jailed. The government could place limits on free speech and the press. Individuals could be imprisoned without being charged with a crime. Some racial or ethnic populations might be singled out and closely watched.

These violations of civil rights have, in fact, occurred in the world's leading democratic countries during natural disasters, civil violence, and international conflicts. Concerns about a nation's security can encourage political leaders to restrict civil rights. Although it does not have to be the case, there is increasing evidence that national security may be a growing threat to civil rights.

Law enforcement uses racial profiling to stop individuals on the street in random searches for drugs and weapons. It is also used to check for suspected terrorists at airports, train stations, and public gathering places. Some profiling only uses racial or ethnic identification for a search. For example, an Arabic name may be enough to profile an individual as a suspected terrorist.

Ethnic and racial profiling

After the shocking acts of terrorist violence against the United States on 9/11, U.S. law enforcement increased the use of ethnic and **racial profiling** in the global war against terrorism. This kind of profiling, an investigation that uses a person's race or ethnic background to decide if the person is likely to commit a crime, has been used in limited ways by governments to check for terrorists, drug users, and other criminals. But it also increases the chances that people will be the target of police or national security investigations because of the color of their skin or their family history. A report by the Lawyers' Committee on Human Rights on events in the aftermath of 9/11, for example, charged that the FBI had detained 1,200 Arabs and other Muslims without it leading to arrests. Most had no access to lawyers and suffered mistreatment, long interrogations, and solitary confinement.

In the United Kingdom, Black drivers are significantly more likely to be stopped by the police than White drivers. In the United States, people with Arab names or who are from the Middle East are more likely to be added to airport "no-fly" lists, which exist to reduce the threat of airline hijackings and terrorism. The theory is that racial profiling may better protect the public from terrorism and crime, but the facts do not yet clearly support the idea. Do you think that racial profiling is a justified violation of personal freedom?

What would you do?

Imagine that you had to make a decision to protect the public from an immediate threat. Which civil rights would you temporarily or permanently reduce to increase public safety? How do you think doing this would help improve public safety? What if there is a threat that could endanger the lives of thousands of people? Would you take away more rights if more people were at risk?

✔ Reduce free speech
✔ Increase secret investigations
✔ Investigate without a warrant
✔ Increase wiretapping
✔ Imprison without a criminal charge
✔ Use harsh interrogation or torture
✔ Call for political assassinations.

> *Civil rights are restricted during national emergencies*

In the global war on terrorism, many countries have restricted the civil rights of individuals charged with terrorist crimes. Unlike regular criminal trials, terrorist defendants may have secret testimony used against them. They may not have the opportunity to identify and challenge witnesses. Confessions that were gained during torture may be used.

Habeas Corpus

Most countries with a historical connection to the United Kingdom use what is known as "common law" as the core of their legal systems. This term relates to laws built up over time based on tradition, custom, and the decisions of judges. One of the most important principles of common law is *habeas corpus*. This is Latin for "We command that you have the body." Under a writ (written request) of *habeas corpus,* a prisoner ("the body") must be brought before a court for it to be proved that he or she is legally detained. In common law countries, *habeas corpus* has become a protection against illegal imprisonment by governments, and a way of safeguarding personal freedom. As the famous 18th-century legal scholar William Blackstone commented in1765, "… it is unreasonable to send a prisoner [to jail], and not to signify withal the crimes alleged against him." Recently, in conflicts involving terrorism in Britain and in the United States, some people have lost this protection.

National security versus civil rights?

National security needs may harm the civil rights gains of the past. But national security, the protection of the public from national and foreign dangers, is necessary to establish and keep civil rights. The primary civil right is the right to life. The government should act to protect the well being of citizens and residents. Restrictions on speech and press freedom for citizens might be necessary to reduce the kind and amount of information that goes to a country's enemies. A violation of a person's privacy by wiretapping their telephone may stop an act of violence and protect the rights of many other people. In addition, when a society is in danger, its participants are less likely to take advantage of or use their rights. The challenge is to decide under what conditions safety is more important than freedom and equality.

Liberty versus safety

"Those who would give up essential Liberty, to purchase a little temporary Safety, deserve neither Liberty nor Safety."

Benjamin Franklin in 1759

"Protecting civil liberties, and people's confidence that those liberties are protected, is a part of protecting national security, just as is the gathering of intelligence to defend us from those who believe it is their duty to make war on us. We have to succeed at both."

U.S. Attorney General and former federal judge Michael Mukasey in October 2007

> *Protection from illegal imprisonment*

One of the great historic violations of civil rights involves the unlawful imprisonment of an individual. "Due process" reforms give defendants the rights that they are "due" under the law, and provide a sense of justice to millions of people. *Habeas corpus* is the protection that a citizen has against a government that tries to hold him or her in jail without a legal charge against them.

 ## U.S. civil rights restrictions that form part of the "War on Terrorism"

✔ The government has expanded powers to stop the publication of documents, reducing a free press.
✔ Citizens can be investigated without a warrant.
✔ The government can wiretap electronic communication in or out of the United States.
✔ A person can be held for months or years in a military camp or prison without a criminal charge.
✔ The government has the power to search a person's rented media and public library records.
✔ Any immigrant can be deported if thought to be a national security risk.
✔ A person can be placed on a no-fly list, preventing him or her from boarding an airplane. This can be based on ethnicity or nationality.

> *Debating improves critical thinking skills*

Training in debate contributes to the intellectual and social development of its participants. Experienced politicians, like California governor Arnold Schwarzenegger, use debating skills as they respond to important political, economic, social, and legal questions.

Debating Civil Rights

The conflict of opinions over civil rights, which has been argued for hundreds of years, continues to this day. Debates on the topic offer an opportunity to research and analyze fundamental questions of equality and liberty. They will help students reveal the best arguments for and against civil rights reforms, as well as develop confidence in expressing powerful opinions about the future of civil rights policy.

Good communication skills help students succeed in classroom discussions and improve their relationships with family and friends. Effective public speakers are able to meet new people, speak in a confident manner, organize a presentation, participate in serious class and community discussions on important topics, and respect the opinions of others.

Persuasive public speakers have the right mix of reasoned arguments and emotional appeals to impress the majority of listeners. They speak with enough volume and emphasis and use eye contact and gestures to connect with an audience.

Debating requires effective public speaking

Good speakers research and know their topics, practice their delivery, and anticipate the argument challenges from an opponent or difficult question from a member of the audience. The best public speakers use many of the same techniques. There is, however, no one best way to deliver a speech. Good speakers are relaxed and communicate to strangers the same and natural way that they might sound when speaking to friends of family, although it may be a bit more formal. There are many choices of format for holding a debate or a discussion. In a discussion panel a group of students participates in a discussion on an issue. Students speak for themselves and may agree or disagree with the opinions of others on the panel. There is an overall time limit, for example, 30 minutes. You can use a moderator to ask questions. Audience questions may be added after the discussion. An open forum is an effective format for a class or large group. A single moderator leads an open discussion on a range of topics. Members of the audience may present new ideas, add to the presentations from others, or refute any issue. The event may last for an hour or more.

Organizing a debate or discussion

Each debate or discussion format has a particular set of rules. You can change rules for the number of participants or amount of time you have available for an event. In a debate one side makes a case for the topic. The other side argues against the case. The side arguing for the topic is called the proposition; the other side is called the opposition. Each speaker on a side delivers a speech. The teams alternate speakers. The proposition team, which must prove that the topic is more likely to be true, speaks first and last. The first opposition speaker refutes the case. Second speakers continue with their team's points and **refute** new points from the other side. The final speeches are summaries of the best arguments for a team. It is possible to add a question and comment time by the opposing side or audience during, in between, or after speeches.

Speakers in a debate

✔ First speaker, proposition – 5 minutes

✔ First speaker, opposition – 5 minutes

✔ Second speaker, proposition – 5 minutes

✔ Second speaker, opposition – 5 minutes

✔ Third speaker, opposition – 3 minutes

✔ Third speaker, proposition – 3 minutes

Debate math

✔ Argument $= A + R + E$
An argument has three parts: assertion, reasoning, evidence.

✔ $X–X = 0$
If an argument has the value of "X" and your opponent argues the opposite, –X, who wins? With zero as the result, neither side wins the point. You must do more than say the opposite of others' opinions to succeed in a debate.

✔ $X–X \; +X+$
Compare your argument with your opponent's. Begin with "X." Your opponent offers the opposite, -X. You defend your argument, adding improved reasons and evidence. Your original argument, X, is now new and improved X+. This is the formula for making a better argument, also what is known as argument extension.

It is possible to have an individual, group, or entire audience judge a debate, voting on the outcome. It is important that judges should not vote for their own opinion on the topic, but rather decide if the proposition proved the case or if the opposition was able to defeat the proposition's arguments.

Some debate formats

Two-sided debate There are two to four students per side and limited time for speeches. The goal is to present a better argument than your opponent on the topic being debated. One side speaks for the topic and one against the topic. Evaluation is usually by a judging panel.

Roundtable discussion In this format there are four to six students on a panel with a limited overall time for discussion. The goal is to inform an audience about the topic and make a good individual showing. A moderator directs the action, with the option of allowing questions from the audience. The audience evaluates the debate.

Open forum Any number can participate in an open forum, however there will need to be a limited overall time for discussion or a specific amount of time for each speaker. The goal is to inform an audience about the topic and make a good individual showing. A moderator is in charge and can allow questions by members of the forum. Evaluation is by a teacher or an expert.

Using one of these formats to debate the success of the civil rights movement will help you understand the issues, evidence, and concerns.
What do you think?

Find Out More

Glossaries

Scholastic civil rights glossary
http://content.scholastic.com/browse/article.jsp?id=4780

Civil Rights Research Center glossary
http://www.civilrights.org/research_center/

Websites

Alabama Department of Archives and History—the Birmingham demonstrations
www.alabamamoments.state.al.us/sec56det.html

Best of History Websites—Civil Rights
www.besthistorysites.net/USHistory_CivilRights.shtml

British Association for American Studies—The Civil Rights Movement
www.baas.ac.uk/resources/pamphlets/pamphdets.asp?id=21

Children of the Movement
www.childrenofthemovement.com/

Civil Rights in Mississippi digital archive
www.lib.usm.edu/~spcol/crda/index.html

Civil rights Movement Veterans
www.crmvet.org

History Now—The Civil Rights Movement
www.historynow.org/06_2006/index.html

PBS—Stand Up For Your Rights
pbskids.org/wayback/civilrights//

So Just
www.sojust.net/

Trenholm Technical Community College Special Collections on Pioneer Civil Rights and Voting Rights Activists
www.trenholmtech.cc.al.us/library/archives

Books

Bausum, Ann. *Freedom Riders: John Lewis and Jim Zwerg on the Front Lines of the Civil Rights Movement.* Washington, D.C.: *National Geographic*, 2005.

Cobb, Charles E., Jr. *On the Road to Freedom: A Guided Tour of the Civil Rights Trial.* Chapel Hill, NC: Algonquin Books, 2008.

Lee, Harper. *To Kill a Mockingbird.* New York: Grand Central Publishing, 1988.

Levine, Ellen. *Freedoms Children*: *Young Civil Rights Activists Tell Their Own Stories*. New York: G.P. Putnam's Sons Books, 2000.

McWhorter, Diane. *A Dream of Freedom*: *The Civil Rights Movement from 1954-1968*. New York: Scholastic, 2004.

There are many autobiographies, memoirs, and biographies of the people involved in the civil rights movement. Look for titles about Martin Luther King, Jr., Bob Marley, Malcolm X, Rosa Parks, Ralph Abernathy, and others.

Documentaries

The Civil Rights Movement (2005)

Color Adjustment (1991)

The Complete Blue Eyed (1998)

Eyes on the Prize (1987)

Foot Soldiers for Equal Justice (2000)

4 Little Girls (1997)

The Rise and Fall of Jim Crow (2002)

Public speaking and debating resources

Comprehensive debate instructions for the classroom and for competitive contests from the Middle School Public Debate Program. www.middleschooldebate.com

Meany, John and Kate Shuster. *Speak Out! Debate and Public Speaking in the Middle Grades,* New York: IDEA Press, 2005.

Glossary

argument statement designed to prove a point. It includes an assertion, reasoning, and evidence (A–R–E).

bias in favor of one particular view or argument

Black Codes laws passed in the former rebel southern states stripping voting rights and other civil rights from freed slaves

Black Panther Party political and social organization that supported civil rights and equality for African Americans and used armed self-defense to guarantee the safety of its members

boycott action that stops consumers from buying or trading, done to influence change

charter document from a ruler or government in which rights and laws are defined, or institutions are legally created

civil disobedience act of protest. Civil disobedience has 3 elements: (1) it is a political act; (2) the act is illegal; and (3) the act is nonviolent.

civil rights opportunities and freedoms that a citizen has under the law. In general, civil rights include voting rights, political freedom, and equality and due process in courts of law.

civil rights movement political movement from the 1940s to the present; it tried to eliminate legal segregation and discrimination

de facto Latin phrase meaning, "by fact." There may be violations of civil rights, despite the civil rights laws that prohibit discrimination. If discrimination exists after the law outlaws it, discrimination is said to be *de facto*, a simple and accurate fact, regardless of the law.

de jure Latin phrase meaning, "by law." It is possible for countries to pass laws that discriminate by using the law.

integration	inclusion of all people in one community, without giving in to a dominant or majority culture or set of customs. Integration was one of the goals of many leaders of the civil rights movement.
Japanese internment	imprisonment of some 120,000 Japanese Americans for national security reasons after the Japanese attack on Pearl Harbor during World War II
Jim Crow laws	discriminatory laws in the U.S. South that segregated races by refusing to permit Blacks to receive the same services in the same way as Whites
Mississippi Freedom Summer Project	campaign during the summer of 1964 using volunteers to register to vote as many unregistered African Americans as possible
pamphleteer	person involved in the writing or publishing of pamphlets
peer	someone of the same age, ability, status, or level of society as another specific person
protest	act of free speech or free action in objection to the way things are. The majority of protests are against unjust policies or leaders.
racial profiling	technique used by police and national security agencies. It uses stereotyping to make an educated guess about who might be likely to commit a crime.
refutation	reply to an argument
segregation	legal separation of the races or other groups. Black Codes and Jim Crow laws are examples of *de jure* segregation.
stereotype	generalized or simplified description of an individual or group by focusing on general impressions, rather than personal detail. They are often negative.
suffragette	woman supporter of the movement to obtain the right to vote for women
universal suffrage	the right of all adults to vote regardless of qualifications such as race, wealth, ethnicity, or religion

Index